THE
2025 Verb Benders Slam Team
Chapbook

BEND 'EM TIL THEY BREAK

Wider Perspectives Publishing ¤ 2025 ¤ Hampton Roads, Va.

Poetry and Writings herein are products of the authors listed with those works and all rights to those works revert to the authors at the time of 1st run/release of this volume. Authors are therefor responsible for distribution and withholding of their works after such time and should be contacted for permission before any repackaging, reproduction, or recirculating of their pieces. Permission granted by one author does not translate to permissions over any other authors' works and the individual authors shall have final control in resubmitting their own work beyond this volume to contests or other anthologies after April 2025.

© April 2025, Hampton Roads, Va., Wider Perspectives Publishing, and respective authors:
Clifford Symay Rhodes including writing as Symay,
Luana Portales including writing as Lu
Stephanie Lask including writing as StephLove
Cassandra Jenkins including writing as Cass IsFree
Madeline Garcia including writing as Maddie G.
J. Scott Wilson including writing as TEECH!
ISBN 978-1-964531-87-8

Contents

Poems by…

Cassandra IsFree	1
Lu	7
Steph Love	17
Maddie G.	25
Symay	33

:Portrayed by
Cassandra Jenkins

Author of
Double Entendre

Quote Me Bish

42

Book of Orgasms

Cassandra Is Free

Double Entendre
~ Cassandra IsFree

Every once in a while, I write a poem and dedicate it to a dead body
They say my words are cold like a dead body
Double entendre
Like I'm cold-blooded in my bluntness
But then I'm cold like how cool I am when I
      blow these bars about Botham, Breonna
Write sonnets to the Sandras
And epithets to the Elijahs
I never wanted to be like Poe
      and have a poem be popular because of its pain
Elizabeth Barrett Browning verses about Mike Brown
I wanted to write like Whitman
But it's too close to White-man, so I guess it's not for me
Gift and the Curse is that I can be a voice,
      but don't get to choose a peaceful pen
No, I write poems dedicated to dead bodies
Bullet riddled
Choked out
Hung juries
In a country where you can't kneel for a black man's rights,
      but on his neck is acceptable
Ironic like separate water fountains
      for the same black women breastfeeding your children
Like you can cook my food but not eat at my table

2025 Verb Benders Slam Team

This is where we live
America
A caricature of human nature
Where the racism booms
And the bodies pile
And I write odes to Oscar Grant and them.

Dope
~ Cassandra IsFree

I said the other day that I wanna quit poetry,
                                                but it won't let me

'Cause behind every black man's last breath is a bar
Every lead from a news story leads to a stanza
Alliterative articles about Afghanistan and the Taliban
Free verse about how they need to free everybody
        locked up over legalized weed

I write trauma in cursive
        while cursing the same hand that feeds me
'Cause these verses are how I eat
And I metaphorically be starving
        for more metaphors to grind with my teeth

It's like planting poetry about grief
Like the hurt is the seed
And the news is the water
The soil is politicians and cops
Dead sons and daughters be the crop
And I make it sound like a field of sunshine
Unintentionally eclipsing the clouds
        And right about now
        It begs the question

2025 Verb Benders Slam Team

When we write poems as an ode
Are we really writing for them or are we writing for tens?

When we say their name what do we hope to gain?
'Cause if we're immortalizing the Trayvons and Atatianas
    for our fame,
        then we're saying it in vain

So when I say I wanna quit poetry
It's not a cry for help or a call to action
It's more like me trying to imagine
Me not being me
Feeling more free to just be Cass
    and less Cassandra IsFree
Like, I'm really locked behind these bars,
    and y'all know the pen means prison
The words are the warden and this is a life sentence

Feels like an addiction

Like I'm getting my high from tryna smoke the competition
And when I come down it's a real low,
    but how can I stay clean if the crowd keeps saying
        I'm dope
So instead of detox I beat box bars about brutality
Converse about calamities, Talk about these tragedies
Detail the disrespect…
    of an officer's knee in a black man's neck

Or better yet, the savagery of shooting
        a young woman in her bed while she rests

        In peace

But I get no sleep cause more incidents with police
        means my poems increase
So when I say I wanna quit poetry but it won't let me
It's because it holds me hostage
In bondage
Chained to a desk by these names like dead weight
I guess it's Stockholm syndrome
        'cause I'm not even trying to escape....

2025 Verb Benders Slam Team

Author of

Mi Casa es Mi Casa

THAT'S LUANA PORTALES

I Left I Rightz
~ Lu

i left my home
To chase a dream
The day i left
My mama cried
She thought that i
Was gonna die
And now i will

Call this poem my speech
Tell them that i
Chase a dream
And cross borders
That lines could never draw
The rally
My figure
My curves
The sit ins
Explaining
Teaching
Loving
That Immigrants are warriors
And sometimes a protest
And sometimes veterans
And sometimes you don't see us in the streets
Because we are boycotting
Target

pull and ship our women
Because our body tea;
but we Boston your party
And refuse to give up

Our seat

In congress
Wearing hoops
So racist comments
　don't bucket
Our mind
is defiant
And we strike
our pose
Because this body
Was born a rebel
A revolution
That doesn't drink lies with ICE
Porque FUCK la migra
And imagine
All the people
Vs
The 1%
Creating a life worth serving
And you know them looks
i be still serving
a country
That fights democracy
Fist up for profit
And defends the oppressor

So here i am
My presence
Is
Resistance
So if
You see me running
And the sirens
Scream
My name
ICE be so violent
They'll call it
a blizzard
So if you see me running
the news using the word criminal as a weapon
Kneel me down
So I looked up to them
So if you see me running
They couldn't bend me
i am American
 revolution as they come
And i
Did not go overseas
To come back to a war
That lacks of civil
And oversees
That i was born with fighting spirit
So if you see me running

Mama mama don't you cry
i left you for a better world

and it wont be long
'Til i get on back home
i got my homies on my tail
Go to war or go to jail
and it wont be long
'Til i get on back home

coLUmbuS PIZArro
~ Lu

I coloniiiiiiiiizzed [English]
     and made it   my own
I tooK a language that is not mía
     and made it feellllllll like home.
I spl   it word   s,
     impregnate(d) them
     & make them sound just like me.
Cris?   Columbus…
     Im biggeRR, badder, and better than him.
I par–t and <u>unite</u> oceans.
     I don't make you pick between
     the boat
     or
     the motion
I let English come
     and go
     as it wants to.
             She my lady, too.
I make my tongue RrroLL, too.
     Let me speak in Tongues for you.
I make English sound brownnnnn.
     My accent a threat
Pum,
     pum,
         pow.
My accent sickkk, mannnn.
     I'm worse than Pizarro.
         I'd do a killing.
     I slit throats and choke them,
         they just trying to say my Last name

Don't call me queen,
       call me *Reyna.*
I conQuered English,
       and I can speak how I want,
       right how I want.
They say I fucked English up,
                    and I didddd.
I made her scream my name, and moan, too.
       Sorry you can't relate to.
They say I make her sound dirty, too.
       I'm not a founding father,
       but She calls me *papi.*
       I bet she don't do that for u.
I make English sound silly and funny, too.
       She a clown, *payaso.*
       She Breaks her own rules.
But I kill,
      kill,
         kill.
I killed the verb to be
      bc I am
           I was and will always be
           hispanic.
My accent ain't nothing, but
      a political act.
My accent so strong:
      It votes
      educates
      and liberates
      the stigma you got on me.
Maybe you don't know,
      but I pain   t,

I make the green-go
    cry and wail.
I painted my passport blue,
    but I got an accent,
    so, that'S not enough for u.
She's not mine or yours.
    She a   hoe.
    She for the people.
    Because we the people.
    It's all of us
Specially if we chew and spit English,
    I want to hear accents so heavy,
    it breaks down discrimination.
        I want to hear accents so thick,
        it switches from bottom to top
        and turns on
            congress for better education.
    I want to hear accents so broad,
    it opens minds, drills Ignorance,
    and doesn't let it become racism.
No espiko inglés.
    Spanglish is my best
    ASSet.
People like me
    build English, too.
I find it revolutionary
    that everyone
    and their mamas
    claimed English to be their native tongue.
When English has never belonged to none
I'm sorry.
    I made English trip

                and fall for me.
English may starve
       if it wasn't for me.
I took English as land,
       Write the will to my kids for me.
Maybe I'm not a colonizer,
maybe my accent is a protest,
       & my pronunciation is reclaiming back
       what it is mine.
I just
       decolonize Englishh
       with my accent
I'm not spicy,
I talk with spice,
       and I defy,
because THIS tongue
       is a movement.
And I dreammmmmm
       that one dayyyyyyy,
            English
            discovers
                     freedom.

Bend 'Em Til They Break

Stephanie Lask
Aka **Steph Love**

Web & Graphic Designer
Slammaster since 2018

Which is to Say
~ Steph Love

I am a poet,
which is to say,
I will overuse any variation of the phrase,
 "which is to say".
But it's only so you can
understand my language,
both literal and figurative.

So, I am a poet,
which is to say,
I overthink every phrase.
Fighting to quiet the whisper
in charge of telling me
I'm not good enough.

In other words,
imposter syndrome,
      is a micromanaging boss
        on your worst day at work.
Imposter syndrome,
      is that hating ass coworker,
        who throws you under the bus,
          but will smile in your face in the break room.

I am a poet,
which is to say,

I suffer from imposter syndrome.
And this office space of a brain
feels like my last write up before termination.

That is to say,
I am to quit before I get fired.
That is to say,
imposter syndrome wants me unemployed.

In other words,
imposter syndrome,
      is being repeatedly told,
      your artistry,
      will never pass the capped starving salary.
Or follow a career path of advancement.

That is to say,
Imposter syndrome,
      is the biggest liar in the boardroom,
      but the truth teller in the morning meetings.
Greeting me with a manipulating grin before I've even had my AM coffee.

I am a poet,
and my poems give me life.
I write myself alive when I don't wish to be.
Use figurative language to uplift myself.
Written reminders that I belong here,
even in the spaces I said I wasn't worthy of.

In other words,
imposter syndrome is the liar.

So, this is the part of the poem,
      where I take back my fire,
      and set a blaze,
      every doubt this monster tried to give me.
When quitting sounded better,
      than succeeding.
When rough times tried to overpower any will I had to keep going.

I am a poet,
which is to say,
I have written my hardships into success stories,
and written myself out of an early grave.

I am a poet,
and I'm still a poet,
even if my pen isn't busy making memorable metaphors.
Maybe it's busy resting.
Trying to recharge itself.

I am a poet,
and sometimes,
it is exhausting to empty your energy,
with no refills.

In other words,
I put everything into every stage.

Every page.
Every mic.
Every night you get this voice.

Wait… lemme rephrase that…

I am a poet,
which is to say,
sometimes,
my words don't believe in me,
but I will rewrite every poem until I change the narrative.

Do you see how being a poet
is grappling with
Imposter syndrome
in it's relentless quest
to kill this part of me?
But, I am a poet,
which means,
every time I die I resurrect myself through my pen.
Breathing life back into my journey.
Because I'm not done talking yet.

So,
I say all that to say.
I am a poet,
and that is to say,
I am,
Immortal.

Tale as Old as Time
~ Steph Love

Beauty and the Beast is a Disney movie
about a girl captured by a beast to save her dad.
This beast, is under a spell from his human form,
And the only way to become himself again
is by getting a kiss
before the last petal
of the enchanted rose falls.

Now, everybody loves a good fairytale,
with that infamous Disney ending.
Rooting for the beast
to change back to human form.
For them to fall in love
and live happily ever after.
A tale as old as time.

I remember when you revealed
your happily ever after.
How perfect the castle was built.
How beautiful the bond.
But when you told me
he hit you,
I immediately thought,
                There falls the first petal.

The beast doesn't always change back to it's human form.
Doesn't know how to control it's rage.
Only knows the chaos in it's claws.
No matter how kind
or giving you are,
this beast
won't change.
Hides his fangs around friends.
Makes himself to be the prince he once was.
                            Another petal drops.

And all we ever want is "what was".
Reflecting on the past
because letting go,
means starting over.
And where is this Belle to go
when she's dealt with enough Gastons
to gaslight her to think she deserves this.
                            There goes another petal

The contents of this castle home,
are all bystanders to his anger.
They've witnessed
the red flag fanfare.
The fists finding a place on your face
afraid you won't see tomorrow.
The simultaneous
screaming for it to stop.
The broken items

making a mess of your relationship.
And you're left with
needing to collect the contents of your brokenness.
Wanting to repair the chip
in your teacup confidence,
to one day be the full China set
you once were.

The time to leave is ticking away like clock's work
I need you to believe in your life's worth
I know that's not slight work
    And another petal
    And another…
    And another…

You never imagined your life
To be a Disney movie
Without the fairytale ending
So when do you choose yourself
Over this tale as old as time?

I can be your guest,
guiding you to overcome
this Stockholm syndrome.
But I fear you won't see
the candlelight,
    before the final petal falls.

2025 Verb Benders Slam Team

Maddie G.

played by Madeline Garcia

Author of **A Vision of She**

Flame of the Forest
~ Maddie G

I am a flame of the forest
and that's a flamboyant Caribbean tree,
rooted in the experiences of those who came before me.
I am an eclectic mix
Of Eurocentric, Africana with an Indigenous twist!
I'm not just some
I am all of it.
My crown,
the first thing you notice about a tree
I am a direct reflection of the fire
ignited at it pith…
The heat on my tongue,
confined between the walls the English language ABCs
putting stops in all my Rs, as if the Ñs I learned as a kid didn't exist.
As if this accent,
was an impediment
because it makes it hard for the white man to understand;
Like I'm not here dominating the English language
while reminding you
my Spanish came first!
My Taino people didn't become extinct
so I would be silent,
they gave me a voice;
A loud bark that serves as a protection
for what resonates inside.
Inside within the collection of rings at the core of this tree.

Each one,
A circle of infinity
knowledge and fight
My ancestor passed down to me
so I may continue our legacy.
So that I
can Poem our narrative into our paper
and not be forced to read how others perceive us to be.
'Cause I am
The Spanish culture that's been infused into our blueprint.
The African resilience that refuses to dissipate in the mix.
The Taino roots that have been planted more than skin deep.
This skin
That's made rough by the stories intertwined to make up our DNA,
this White privilege that gets canceled out
by our black and indigenous heritage,
forced to conform…
But not my abuela…. You see,
My grandma still refuses to stop speaking her native tongue.
To some, it may rebellion
but to her, is her only hope
so that the substance of who we are
is not totally lost.
If you listen to her words
they will always be encoded
with the coordinates of home.
Like always asking my abuelita for la bendición,
with a kiss on my forehead
to let me know,
God will always guide me

because that is what she asked for
in every oración.
And as I grow old,
I know my branches
will not have my abuelita
to bless them on
as it will be my turn;
And In my grandkids broken Spanish
it will sound more like "cion pita".
And with a smile
I will always respond:
"Dios les bendiga, vayan con Dios"
In other words,
what I want my leaves to know
is that as you grow further from my trunk
You are Me...
You and I
are We!
That I know traditions will evolve,
that we will always mix the new with a little bit of the old
but ultimately out essence will forever live on.
That even when you no longer speak Español
you will always bear traces of the history
that run through your blood.
That even when you decide to go out there
and grow a forest of your own
never forget...
You are part of this tree
Made of all of us!!!!

Who am I?
~ Maddie G

I come from a seed imported from a far away land
To satisfy the colonizers curiosity
      of what could blossom from the inside.
Yet my kind will forever be unknown
strange fruit that will never be understood.
'Cause I'm a contradiction of what they see
      versus what I taste like
bewitching the palate
convincing the brain
the eyes have been lying since the beginning of time
I am a flower
that was deemed to bloom in any garden
even a concrete one
like a parasite that attaches to its surroundings
      in order not to die.
Survival of the fittest
I Gloria Gaynor the shit out of this life…
I am a survivor.
A child destined to thrive to be remembered
Words I immortalized in this poem
      so I never forget
      I have to stay working hard.
You see,
they keep pushing back the finish line
thinking giving up will be my only choice
they keep forgetting where I come from

That I am as much colonizer
      as I am Taino
           as I am slave
I can muscle my way to the finish line
      or verbally slap you with my intellect
           En Espanol y en Ingles
Yes!!!
I get tongue twisted time and again
That's from all the verbs I have
      bending in my head
I can call you hijo eh puta…. or son of a bitch,
      All in one breath
I'm sorry… Excuse me!
I keep forgetting what I was gonna say next….. Concentrate
I am concentrated coffee before it became Americanized
Café Dominicano
Like the Caribbean sun I shine
I am
Black girl magic
passed down from my black grandma through my white mom.
To get a clear picture
a mix of different races
that is how Dominican I am
I AM
The dopest line in the poem that makes you want to say rewind
I am the exact vision of the future
my ancestors had
I'm the point of reference
Next Generation will look back at
I am a mother, a daughter, a poet, a sister, a friend

I'm a work in progress
I am the promise I made to my past
      that my future would be great.
In the present,
I am still downloading
And I can't wait to show you what I have coming up next…

Bend 'Em Til They Break

Clifford Symay Rhodes
as
PROFESSOR SYMAY

Wrote the treatise :

Poetry is Like Medicine

Hands
~ Symay

Ever since I could remember
I've never known what to do with my hands

They search for braille along the air
Attempting to read the room
They know 25 letters of the alphabet
No, 26
It's hard for me to recognize the cues
It's like they know every sign but stop
My hands shake before hand shakes
And keeping things together feels like holding on to tectonic plates
And I thought it was just me

Until my 8th grade mentee comes up to me
He says
There's a dance on Friday
I've got everything covered…except
When dancing with a girl
What do you do with your hands

I tell him
Stay at the hips
You will have the urge to raise them
Do not
If she is dancing with you she trust you
Enough to feel the root of her motion

You will have the urge to slide down
Do not
Though you have been invited to the door
It does not mean enter unannounced
Do not hold on too lightly
You must be the road paved enough for her to walk upon
Do not hold on too tightly
Though the road is paved
She must be free enough to chose it for herself
But at all times
Be ready
To let go
Because you are more focused
       on what you are doing with your hands
Than what you have in them
You have missed their function
So go
Let fun replace fear
Have a good time

Right then I realize
There is something I forgot to tell him

When you are walking home
Hopefully off the bliss of your first kiss
There is a chance you are stopped by police
And awkward blue boys have history
Of not knowing what to do with their hands

They place their hands on holsters
       to keep them from dancing
But trigger fingers start toe tapping
Itching to pull a partner
When they ask you to dance
Keep your hands
Shoulder height
You will have the urge to raise them
Do not
Because raised hands are a means to strike
And a sign of surrender
You cannot control how your message is received
You will have the urge to slide down
Do not
Because that looks like reaching
For weapon or ID
For they have weaponized identity
So when they tell you to interlock those fingers
Do not
Hold on to your blackness to tightly
When they attempt cuff you
Do not
Hold on to your submission too lightly
Because they can be so distracted
       by what you are doing with your hands
They don't notice your life in theirs

So I want to pray
I want to fight
I want to reach
I want to throw my hands in the air and give up
But, I still
Never know what to do with my hands

Feathers
~ Symay

Question posed to my 6th grade English class

"Why is hope the thing with feathers"

Answers include:

It's foul
It gets plucked

everyday
we duck

playing chicken
Running

Head of household
Cut-off

Robbin' vest chested
Eagles fly

Over deserted desert
Isles

can't find food
First thing in morning

Teacher says smile
I ain't ate since lunch

Yesterday
Mama had to be convinced to call cops

Pop's hits land surprise
Sunken in jaw drops

Rather be snitch
Than my siblings see sickness

Mama sad
Relationship wrecked

We stranded
In the middle

Of an ocean of bills
and a concrete jungle

ready to swing
on everything

because Lord know we pray down here

hope is the thing with feathers
I've only seen

wings
On obituaries and T-shirts

Bend 'Em Til They Break

2025 Verb Benders Slam Team

Just So's You Know the Score
~ TEECH!

You asked, "Do I have the time?"

Yeah
I keep the time
and I attack with the plus sign

Don't need depth with me
While I'm not exercising real authority
More: staving off the long, cold lonely
Finding a passion as something of a non-entity
I act like I'm the stumbling block
  No, you cannot walk past me
  and just spit poetry
I catch light, I have density, exude gravity,
I'm made of matter, I matter, see!?

You think you're just gonna go home
Wash off and get stoned?
And that I just *Wrote* this poem?!
  BUT
Standing in judgment before these
  numbers can be your rut
I see you in the back, pacing, shy
"*Am I ready?*" thoughts play deep in your gut
Hey, if you want numbers ten feet high
  I'm your guy!
It's how I plain-sight hide!

www.ingramcontent.com/pod-product-compliance
Lightning Source LLC
Chambersburg PA
CBHW071752090426
42738CB00011B/2653